D1626663

FASCINATING
BIBLE FACTS
VOL. 1

FASCINATING BIBLE FACTS

VOL. 1

103 DEVOTIONS

IRENE HOWAT

Published by
Christian Focus Publications,
Geanies House, Fearn, Tain, Ross-shire,
IV20 1TW, Scotland, U.K.

www.christianfocus.com
email: info@christianfocus.com

Cover design by Thomas Barnard
Illustrations by Tim Charnick
Printed and bound in Europe

For my friend Jean,
with thanks.

Contents

GET STARTED

Here are 103 facts for you to discover about God and his Word – the Bible.

Look out for the Fact Finders: Chloe, Zac and Abbi. Chloe has questions, Zac is ready with a challenge or two and Abbi has some useful information to add to all the facts

After each fact there is a promise from God. These promises are repeated in slightly different words and in different places in the Bible.

Chloe   Zac   Abbi

Look out for Chloe, Zac and Abbi throughout the book.

WHAT IS A FACT?

A fact is something that is certain, sure and true, something so reliable that we can use it as the basis of our lives. The Bible is true because it is the Word of God and God cannot tell lies. Therefore all the stories quoted in this book are factual and true.

Fascinating Bible Facts Vol. 1 also includes many promises of God. But how can promises be facts? They can when God makes them! When we make a promise we try to keep it, but the Lord is so wonderful that all his promises are as good as kept the moment he makes them. So the promises of God are facts – certain, sure and true – and we can safely base our lives on them. God the Lord will never, ever, ever let us down.

FLYING THINGS

1 The Bible is an amazing book that teaches us about the past, the present and the future. One of the things that took place in the past is creation. Did you know that God made birds  and animals on a different day? He did. The Lord created birds and fish on the fifth day of creation and animals and man on the sixth day. (Genesis 1:20-23)

When Noah and his family were in the ark the rain fell for forty days and nights. For the next 150 days the depth of water gradually went down until the bottom of the ark settled on top of Mount Ararat. Noah waited for another forty days before opening the window of the ark and letting a raven loose. The raven didn't return to the ark and Noah sent out a dove.

• •

BIBLE PROMISE: 'For God so loved the world that he gave his only begotten Son, that whoever believes in him shall not perish but have eternal life' (John 3:16).

2 The dove flew all around but couldn't find anywhere to land. That told Noah that there was still water all over the earth and that it was too soon to think about releasing his precious cargo of God's creatures. (Genesis 8:6-9)

Just one week later, Noah set the same dove free again. After a while, the bird returned with a freshly-plucked olive leaf in its beak! How excited Noah must have been to discover that the water had gone down so far that there were trees to be seen once again. The next week, he set the dove free once again and that was the last he saw of it. Noah knew the time would soon come to set his living cargo loose on dry land once again. (Genesis 8:10-14)

• •

BIBLE PROMISE: 'I the LORD do not change' (Malachi 3:6).

3 Three of the plagues the Lord sent on Pharaoh and the Egyptian people were flying things: gnats, flies and locusts. Pharaoh's magicians knew that it was God who had sent all these creatures, but Pharaoh still wouldn't let the Israelite people go. What a hard-hearted man he was!

The wonder was that, as soon as Moses prayed to the Lord to remove the plagues, not a single one of the pests remained! (Exodus 8:16-32)

. . . .

ABBI'S INFO: Pharaoh's magicians tried to do the same things as Moses with their secret magic. When they tried this they never really succeeded. In fact sometimes they made things worse. Read Exodus chapter 7.

BIBLE PROMISE: Jesus said, 'I will ask the Father, and he will give you another Counsellor to be with you for ever – the Spirit of truth' (John 14:16).

4 After God rescued his people from Egyptian slavery, Moses led them through the wilderness towards the Promised Land. Before long the people were moaning about their dull diet. What did they expect in a wilderness? God did an amazing thing. He sent a great number of quail (small edible birds) to the Israelite camp, enough to feed all the people. Although they didn't deserve it one little bit, God still cared for them. (Exodus 16:13)

God looked after his people so carefully. He used a wonderful expression to describe his care of his people. He told Moses, '... I carried you on eagles' wings and brought you to myself.' (Exodus 19:4)

• •

BIBLE PROMISE: 'And we know that in all things God works for the good of those who love him, who have been called according to his purpose' (Romans 8:28).

5 Elijah was one of God's greatest prophets. He was sent by the Lord to a water brook, but there was no food there for him to eat. The Lord made an amazing thing happen. Each day he sent ravens carrying bread and meat to Elijah, and not just once a day. The ravens arrived with food for him every morning and every evening. God provided water for Elijah from the brook and food by raven air-mail! (1 Kings 17:1-6)

Elijah didn't need to worry, for the Lord was looking after him. However, Jesus knows that people worry about things.

● ●

BIBLE PROMISE: 'You are all sons of God through faith in Christ Jesus ...' (Galatians 3:26).

6 Once, when Jesus was talking about worry, he reminded the great crowd around him that they should not worry because God cares for them. The picture he used to teach them that lesson was birds flying in the air. They don't plant seeds or harvest crops, but God provides for them. Jesus said, people are much more valuable than birds! (Matthew 6:25-27)

Some time later the Lord said that we are of more worth than many sparrows. Then he went on to tell us a fascinating fact – God cares for us so much that he knows how many hairs each of us has on our head! (Matthew 10:29-30)

BIBLE PROMISE: 'He who dwells in the shelter of the Most High will rest in the shadow of the Almighty' (Psalm 91:1).

7 In the days before clocks, people knew the time by various signs of nature, like the rising of the sun and the cockerel's morning crow.

The night on which Jesus was arrested, Peter said that he would never disown the Lord. Jesus knew better and he told Peter that he would disown him three times before the cockerel crowed.

And the fascinating fact? Jesus knew what was happening in Peter's heart and what would happen in the future. (Matthew 26:31-35, 69-75)

• •

BIBLE PROMISE: 'Blessed are the peacemakers, for they will be called sons of God' (Matthew 5:9).

WATER EVERYWHERE!

8 We find water at the beginning of the Bible and at the end. Water was one of the first parts of God's creation, (Genesis 1:1-2) and all of creation is dependent on it. There would be no animals, no birds, certainly no fish and definitely no you if the Lord had not first made water. The Bible ends with water in Revelation 22.

The gospel is an invitation to come to faith in Jesus who is the living water. Until the Lord comes back in glory, people will be invited to believe in him. God's Word says, '"Come!" Whoever is thirsty, let him come; and whoever wishes, let him take the free gift of the water of life' (Revelation 22:17). Have you done that yet?

• •

BIBLE PROMISE: Jesus says, 'I am the bread of life. He who comes to me will never go hungry, and he who believes in me will never be thirsty' (John 6:35).

9 The Garden of Eden was a beautiful place and things grew wonderfully well there. No wonder, it was watered by its own special river. (Genesis 2:10)

Thorns and thistles also grow where ground is well watered. One of the wonderful facts about Eden was that there were no thorns and thistles in it at all. They were nowhere to be seen until after Adam and Eve had sinned. (Genesis 3:17-18)

• •

CHLOE'S QUESTIONS: What did the dove have in its beak when it returned to the ark?

BIBLE PROMISE: 'Because he (Jesus) himself suffered when he was tempted, he is able to help those who are being tempted' (Hebrews 2:18).

10

God's people were slaves in Egypt for many years. When they were eventually freed by Pharaoh, they were hardly out of the land when he changed his mind and sent his troops to recapture them.

The Hebrew people were just coming to the Red Sea when Pharaoh and his soldiers came up behind them! God's people had the sea in front of them and soldiers behind, but that wasn't a problem for the Lord. He opened up a dry path right across the sea and the Hebrews were able to walk straight through it – with walls of water on either side. (Exodus 14)

● ●

CHLOE'S QUESTIONS: What flying creature brought food to Elijah?

BIBLE PROMISE: God says, 'Do not be afraid; you will not suffer shame. Do not fear disgrace; you will not be humiliated' (Isaiah 54:4).

11 The waters closed in on the Egyptians and they were drowned. (Exodus 14:15-28) Believe it or not, just three days after the Hebrew people were free of Pharaoh forever they were grumbling and complaining to Moses because they had nothing to drink.

God led them to water at a place called Marah ... and it tasted disgusting! The Lord showed Moses how to make the water taste good and then used that as a lesson to the people. If they kept God's commands, he would look after them. (Exodus 15:22-26)

. . . .

ZAC'S CHALLENGE: Read the verse below. Draw a picture of what it makes you think of.

BIBLE PROMISE: 'For the LORD God is a sun and shield; the Lord bestows favour and honour; no good thing does he withhold from those whose walk is blameless' (Psalm 84:11).

12 There was another time when the Israelites were thirsty for lack of water. They complained to Moses, even saying that they would have been better off staying in Egypt! Moses went to the Lord and complained about the people!

God told Moses to strike a rock with his stick and that water would come gushing out of it. That's exactly what happened. Did that stop the people complaining? Only for a short time. Typical! (Exodus 17:1-7)

BIBLE PROMISE: 'As long as the earth endures, seedtime and harvest, cold and heat, summer and winter, day and night will never cease' (Genesis 8:22).

13

When King Saul was chasing David for his life, David sometimes had the opportunity to kill Saul, but he didn't. Once he came upon King Saul's camp when everyone was asleep. He crept up to the king and took away the spear and water jug from right beside his head. He could just as easily have thrust the spear through Saul. Then David went a short distance away and shouted to Saul's army telling them what he had done. Saul realised that he was doing wrong.

When David gave the king back his spear, he explained that he could not kill the man whom God had made king over them. Sadly, Saul was not sorry for long and was soon back chasing David and trying to kill him. (1 Samuel 26:7-25)

BIBLE PROMISE: '… the Lord your God is gracious and compassionate' (2 Chronicles 30:9).

14

What would you not do if you wanted something to burn? You wouldn't soak it with water.

Elijah and the prophets of the idol, Baal, agreed to meet on Mount Carmel. They were going to call on their idol to burn their sacrifice and then Elijah was going to call on the Lord God to burn his one.

The prophets of Baal prayed and screamed and yelled all day, but nothing happened. Elijah soaked ... really soaked ... his sacrifice and the ground all around it before praying.

The Lord answered his prayers and sent fire to burn up his sacrifice. Not only that, but God's fire dried up every drop of water too! (1 Kings 18:16-39)

• •

BIBLE PROMISE: God's 'dominion is an everlasting dominion that will not pass away, and his kingdom is one that will never be destroyed' (Daniel 7:14).

15

The mystery of floating metal! Elisha was one of the great Old Testament prophets. Some of the men who were learning from him decided to build a place where they could all live together.

As one of them was cutting down a tree, the iron head came off the axe he was using and fell into the River Jordan. The man was very upset because he had borrowed the axe. Elisha asked where it had fallen and then threw a stick into the river near the place to which the man pointed. When he did that, the iron axe head floated up to the surface of the water and the man was able to lift it out! With God all things are possible. (2 Kings 6:1-7)

BIBLE PROMISE: Jesus said, 'Whoever welcomes this little child in my name welcomes me; and whoever welcomes me welcomes the one who sent me. For he who is least among you all – he is the greatest' (Luke 9:48).

16

Would you like to be blessed by God? The very first psalm says that the person who is blessed delights in God's Word rather than in the company of sinful people doing sinful things. And those who delight in God's Word are like trees planted by streams of water. They have lovely leaves and they bear fruit too. (Psalm 1:3)

The fruit that God grows in the lives of his people is love, joy, peace, patience, kindness, goodness, faithfulness, gentleness and self-control. (Galatians 5:22-23)

•••••••••••••••••••••••••••••••••

BIBLE PROMISE: 'The LORD is faithful to all his promises and loving towards all he has made. The LORD upholds all those who fall and lifts up all who are bowed down' (Psalm 145:13-14).

17 There was once a man who loved and served the Lord. His name was Job and, despite his faith, he had a really hard time. He lost his family, his wealth and even his health. Not only that, he had some awful 'friends' who thought it was their business to tell him it was all his fault!

Eventually, God spoke to Job. He pointed out the wonders of creation. God asked, 'Can you raise your voice to the clouds and cover yourself with a flood of water? Do you send the lightning bolts on their way?' Of course he didn't! And when Job looked away from his own problems to the wonders of God's creation he began to feel better. (Job 38:34-35)

When you feel down, ask the Lord to help you to look away from your problems to the wonderful things he has made. That will help you to put things in perspective.

BIBLE PROMISE: 'No temptation has seized you except what is common to man. And God is faithful; he will not let you be tempted beyond what you can bear' (1 Corinthians 10:13).

18 There are times when life is really hard for the Christian as well as for the unbeliever. Faith is not a vaccine to protect us against life. But God has a wonderful watery promise for his people. 'When you pass through the waters, I will be with you; and when you pass through the rivers, they will not sweep over you' (Isaiah 43:2). And God keeps all his promises.

• •
BIBLE PROMISE: 'Then the land will yield its harvest, and God, our God, will bless us. God will bless us, and all the ends of the earth will fear him' (Psalm 67:6-7).

19

Jonah knew all about water!

He brought his problems on himself by being really stupid. Jonah thought he could run away from God – as though anyone could run that fast! The wonderful thing is that the Lord still forgave Jonah, even though he was deliberately sinful.

Sometimes we sin without knowing it, but God the Lord is so gracious that he even forgives our deliberate sins when we ask for his mercy. (Read the whole Book of Jonah which is found between Obadiah and Micah.)

BIBLE PROMISE: 'Just as man is destined to die once, and after that to face judgment, so Christ was sacrificed once to take away the sins of many people; and he will appear a second time, not to bear sin, but to bring salvation to those who are waiting for him' (Hebrews 9:27-28).

20

Do you ever wish that everyone in the world knew about the Lord Jesus? The prophet Habakkuk tells of a great day when 'the earth will be filled with the knowledge of the glory of the Lord, as the waters cover the sea.' (Habakkuk 2:14)

A day will come when even those who have no Christian faith will discover the glory of God.

Sadly, when that day does come, it will be too late for them to repent and go to heaven.

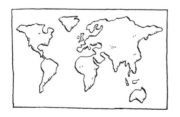

BIBLE PROMISE: 'You are awesome, O God, in your sanctuary; the God of Israel gives power and strength to his people. Praise be to God!' (Psalm 68:35).

21 The Lord Jesus' first miracle involved water. He was at a wedding when the wine ran out. Jesus turned ordinary water into the best of wine, so good that the people who drank it noticed the difference and commented on it. (John 2:1-11)

Does that mean that we can drink as much wine as we like? No, because elsewhere in the Bible we are told, 'Do not get drunk on wine' (Ephesians 5:18). There should be no such thing as a drunk Christian.

• •

BIBLE PROMISE: 'How much more, then, will the blood of Christ, who through the eternal Spirit offered himself unblemished to God, cleanse our consciences from acts that lead to death, so that we may serve the living God!' (Hebrews 9:14).

22 One day, Jesus and his friends were out in a boat when a terrible storm blew up, so terrible that even his professional fishermen friends were scared out of their minds. The Lord Jesus commanded the wind to stop blowing and the waves to be still ... and the wind did stop blowing and the waves became still! (Matthew 8:23-27)

Do you believe that? You should. It's in the Bible, which is the Word of God, and God doesn't tell lies.

• •

CHLOE'S QUESTIONS: What was Jesus' first miracle?

BIBLE PROMISE: Jesus said of those who believe in him – 'I have come that they may have life, and have it to the full' (John 10:10).

23 Jesus went on to a hillside to pray and his friends set out home by boat. When a storm blew up he went to them – walking on the surface of the water. At first his friends thought he was a ghost, but then they recognised Jesus. Peter – always the impulsive one – asked if he could walk on the water to meet Jesus. He did, and he didn't sink until he took his eyes off the Lord. (Matthew 14:22-33)

If we keep our eyes on Jesus as we find him in the Bible, he will help us not to sink into fearfulness and sin.

● ●

BIBLE PROMISE: Jesus says, 'Come to me, all you who are weary and burdened, and I will give you rest' (Matthew 11:28).

24

Do you know the fascinating fact that there is special water that never leaves us thirsty again?

Jesus used the picture of water to tell a sinful woman that he could supply all her spiritual needs for time and for eternity. He said, '… whoever drinks the water I give him will never thirst. Indeed, the water I give him will become in him a spring of water welling up to eternal life' (John 4:14).

Jesus himself is the water of life and the only one who can satisfy the needs of our souls.

• •

ZAC'S CHALLENGE: Jesus is described in many ways. Look up these verses John 4:14, John 6:35, John 8:12; John 10:11; John 15:1; 1 Corinthians 10:4. Draw a picture of each item.

BIBLE PROMISE: '… if you confess with your mouth, "Jesus is Lord," and believe in your heart that God raised him from the dead, you will be saved' (Romans 10:9).

25

Jesus met a man in Jerusalem who had been disabled for thirty-eight years. He was lying beside a special pool of water that had healing powers, but the man could not get to the water and had nobody to help him.

Jesus asked the man if he wanted to be healed. Imagine asking him that! However, Jesus was asking the man if he really wanted to take on all the responsibilities of good health. He'd had everything done for him for thirty-eight long years. The Lord really understood what was in his heart. The disabled man did want to be well and Jesus healed him right away. Jesus understands your heart too. (John 5:1-9)

• •

BIBLE PROMISE: 'The LORD is good to those whose hope is in him, to the one who seeks him; it is good to wait quietly for the salvation of the LORD. It is good for a man to bear the yoke while he is young' (Lamentations 3:25-27).

2 6 On the night before Jesus died, he did an amazing thing. He and his friends met for a special meal. The tradition was that someone washed the feet of those who gathered to eat. However, this time nobody was willing to do it, so Jesus took off his outer clothes, wrapped a towel around himself, took a bowl of water and washed his friends' feet, including the feet of Judas.

Jesus, who is Almighty God, humbled himself to wash his betrayer's feet. And he humbled himself to wash our hearts free from sin. (John 13:1-17)

• •

BIBLE PROMISE: God says, 'Then you will call upon me and come and pray to me, and I will listen to you' (Jeremiah 29:12).

27 The Apostle Paul got into deep water – quite literally.

When he was being taken as a prisoner to Rome, the ship he was in was caught in a terrible storm. God told Paul to tell the sailors that nobody would be drowned (although the ship would be lost) if they did as he told them.

That's exactly what happened. The ship was smashed to pieces, but every single person on board was washed safely on to the coast of Malta. (Acts 27:27-44)

● ●

CHLOE'S QUESTION: Who walked on the water with Jesus?

BIBLE PROMISE: 'The LORD will fulfil his purpose for me; your love, O LORD, endures for ever – do not abandon the works of your hands' (Psalm 138:8).

28

In the new young church in Corinth people started arguing over which of the great preachers to follow. Imagine that!

Paul wrote them a serious letter telling them that the new church was like a garden and the preachers were like gardeners. Some planted seeds (preached the gospel) and others watered the ground (taught the new Christians), but only God could make the seed of faith grow in their hearts. (1 Corinthians 3:3-9)

It can be tempting to idolise great Christians, but our one and only true hero is Jesus.

BIBLE PROMISE: 'Good will come to him who is generous and lends freely, who conducts his affairs with justice' (Psalm 112:5).

GETTING AROUND

2 9 **WALKING** – Probably the most exciting walk ever was from Jerusalem to Emmaus. It took place the day Jesus rose from the dead. Two men, who loved the Lord, were walking to Emmaus. As they walked, they talked about the awful things that had happened to their friend Jesus on the cross. A man joined them and asked what they were talking about.

Only when they arrived at their destination, and invited the stranger in for a meal, did they realise that he wasn't a stranger at all. He was the risen Lord Jesus! (Luke 24:13-35)

• •

BIBLE PROMISE: God told Moses, 'Now go; I will help you speak and will teach you what to say' (Exodus 4:12). And to his friends whose faith would be challenged, Jesus said, '...do not worry about how you will defend yourselves or what you will say, for the Holy Spirit will teach you at that time what you should say' (Luke 12:11-12).

30

ON A CHARIOT – When God released the Hebrew people from their slavery in Egypt, they escaped on foot. Soon afterwards Pharaoh decided to go after them and sent his troops, many of them on chariots, to recapture their slaves. But although the Hebrews were walking and their enemies were on chariots, they were safe in the hands of God.

The Lord opened up the Red Sea for his people to cross over and closed it again on the Egyptians, horses, chariots and all. (Exodus 14:5-29)

• •

BIBLE PROMISE: 'The LORD is a refuge for the oppressed, a stronghold in times of trouble' (Psalm 9:9).

31

RUNNING – Even God's great prophets were human, and when they forgot how wonderful the Lord is, they lost for a time their gift of peace.

Elijah had just won an amazing victory over idol worshippers when tiredness and emotion got the better of him. In 1 Kings 19:3 we find him running away for his life.

God knew what his servant had been through and dealt very tenderly with him. The whole story is told in 1 Kings 19.

BIBLE PROMISE: Jesus said, 'I will not leave you as orphans; I will come to you' (John 14:18).

32

LIMPING – Mephibosheth was quite the opposite of Elijah. He couldn't run at all because he had been disabled by an accident in childhood.

David and Jonathan had been very good friends and Mephibosheth was Jonathan's son. For the sake of the love he had had for Jonathan, King David showed kindness to Mephibosheth for the rest of his life. (2 Samuel 9)

Even kings should be looking out for ways of serving people, rather than always being served.

· ·

ABBI'S INFO: King David set an example of being kind of someone who was disabled. Are we kind to people who are a little different from us?

BIBLE PROMISE: 'Do not be anxious about anything, but in everything, by prayer and petition, with thanksgiving, present your requests to God. And the peace of God, which transcends all understanding, will guard your hearts and your minds in Christ Jesus' (Philippians 4:6-7).

3 3 **CARRIED** – Another man in the Bible was even more disabled. He couldn't walk at all.

Four friends tried to get him to Jesus for healing. As the house the Lord was in was crowded, the men carried their friend up the steps on to the flat roof and then broke through it, lowering their friend's stretcher to Jesus, and watched in delight as he was healed! (Mark 2:1-12)

• •

ABBI'S INFO: In Bible times, and even today in Middle eastern countries, roofs are often flat because in dry hot countries people don't need to have sloping roofs to let the rain run off. This meant it was easier for the friends in the story to gain access to the house.

BIBLE PROMISE: Jesus said, 'Ask and it will be given to you; seek and you will find; knock and the door will be opened to you. For everyone who asks receives; he who seeks finds, and to him who knocks, the door will be opened' (Matthew 7:7-8).

34

ON A DONKEY – When the Lord Jesus Christ was entering Jerusalem, knowing that he would die soon after he arrived there, he rode on a donkey. Just imagine the scene, the Lord being taken slowly through the excited crowds, many of whom had cut down palm branches to place on the road before him. Not only that, but they shouted praise to the Lord as he passed by. (Matthew 21:6-10)

Sadly, not many days later, some of the same people called out for his crucifixion.

. . . .

BIBLE PROMISE: 'The Lord gives strength to his people; the Lord blesses his people with peace' (Psalm 29:11).

3 5

WALKING ON WATER – Remember the night Jesus walked on water to the boat his friends were in? He was able to do that because he made everything, and creation does exactly what Jesus tells it to do. (Matthew 14:22-36)

• •

ABBI'S INFO: When Jesus walked on the water it was the fourth watch of the night – this means it was between 3 am and 6 am.

BIBLE PROMISE: Jesus said, 'I tell you the truth, whoever hears my word and believes him who sent me has eternal life and will not be condemned; he has crossed over from death to life' (John 5:24).

36

ON A SHIP – Paul, who was the most famous of the early missionaries, got into serious trouble for his preaching. So much so, that he was taken to Rome (the capital of the Empire) to stand trial. To get there he had to sail across the Mediterranean Sea to Italy – being shipwrecked on Malta on the way! (Acts 27)

• •

ZAC'S CHALLENGE: Where on the map is the Mediterranean Sea?

BIBLE PROMISE: 'The lions may grow weak and hungry, but those who seek the LORD lack no good thing' (Psalm 34:10).

37

IN A WHIRLWIND – The prophet Elijah knew it was nearing the time when he would leave earth and go home to heaven. But I don't think he would ever have guessed how he would get there.

As he and Elisha 'were walking and talking together, suddenly a chariot of fire and horses of fire appeared and separated the two of them, and Elijah went up to heaven in a whirlwind' (2 Kings 2:11). Elijah was given the great blessing of not having to die before going to heaven.

• •

BIBLE PROMISE: God says, 'Call to me and I will answer you and tell you great and unsearchable things you do not know' (Jeremiah 33:3).

MEALS THAT MATTERED

38 Abraham's twin grandsons, Esau and Jacob, were never really friends. Esau was the older – just! And in those days that was very important.

Once after they were grown up, Esau came home very hungry and asked Jacob for some of the stew he had made. Jacob, a cheat if ever there was one, said he could have the stew if he gave away all his rights as older son. Esau did that!

Things went from bad to worse between them from then on. (Genesis 25:24-34)

●●●●●●●●●●●●●●●●●●●●●●●●●●●●●●●●●

CHLOE'S QUESTIONS: Who should be our one true hero?

BIBLE PROMISE: Jesus said, 'Everything is possible for him who believes' (Mark 9:23).

39

Joseph, who was sold into Egyptian slavery by his brothers, had a splendid opportunity to get his own back on them.

God had blessed him, and he'd been promoted to high position in Egypt. When a famine hit that part of the world Joseph was in charge of food distribution ... and his brothers came to buy some!

What happened then is complicated but, eventually, over a meal, he told them who he was and assured them that they were forgiven. (Genesis 45:1-7)

Having the opportunity of repaying one bad turn with another doesn't mean we should do it!

. . . .

BIBLE PROMISE: 'The Lord redeems his servants; no-one who takes refuge in him will be condemned' (Psalm 34:22).

40

When the time came for God to free the Hebrews from their slavery in Egypt, he gave Moses very strict instructions what to do. Each Hebrew family had to kill a lamb and paint its blood around the door frames of their houses. They were then to eat the roasted lamb and prepare to leave Egypt.

That night the Lord took the life of the firstborn son in every home where there was no blood on the door, passing over the Hebrew homes. That's why it was called the Passover. Even to this day Jewish people celebrate the Passover every year. (Exodus 12:1-30)

BIBLE PROMISE: 'For I am the LORD, your God, who takes hold of your right hand and says to you, Do not fear; I will help you' (Isaiah 41:13).

41 Elijah, that brave prophet of God, had many difficult times, especially when King Ahab was on the throne. Once, Elijah had to give bad news from the Lord to Ahab. He had to tell him that for three years there would be no rain on the land, not even any dew in the mornings! Having told the king, God's servant had to leave the area ... quickly. The Lord led him to a place called Kerith, where there was a brook from which he could drink. (1 Kings 17:1-6)

CHLOE'S QUESTIONS: Who travelled up to heaven in a whirlwind?

BIBLE PROMISE: Jesus said, 'My sheep listen to my voice; I know them, and they follow me. I give them eternal life, and they shall never perish; no-one can snatch them out of my hand. My Father, who has given them to me, is greater than all; no-one can snatch them out of the Father's hand. I and the Father are one' (John 10:27-30).

54

42

When the brook dried up, God told Elijah to go to Zarephath where a widowed woman would look after him. But the woman had only enough for one meal for herself and her son and then they expected to die!

Here's what Elijah told her. 'Don't be afraid. Go home and do as you have said. But first make a small cake of bread for me from what you have and bring it to me, and then make something for yourself and your son. For this is what the Lord, the God of Israel says: "The jar of flour will not be used up and the jug of oil will not run dry until the day the Lord gives rain on the land"' (1 Kings 17:13-14). And that's exactly what happened!

BIBLE PROMISE: 'Even youths grow tired and weary, and young men stumble and fall; but those who hope in the LORD will renew their strength. They will soar on wings like eagles; they will run and not grow weary, they will walk and not be faint' (Isaiah 40:30-31).

43

Daniel and his three friends were just young men when they were captured and taken to Babylon. The King of Babylon wanted to train them up to work for him and he gave them the very best of food and wine from his own table.

Daniel, who trusted the Lord, wasn't going to be bought by fine food. The four friends asked for a simple vegetarian diet and were given it for a ten day trial period. At the end of the ten days they looked so well on it that they were allowed to continue! (Daniel 1:11-16)

ABBI'S INFO: Daniel's friends were called Shadrach, Meshach and Abednego. But these names were their Babylonian names given to them after their capture. At home in Israel they were called Hananiah, Mishael and Azariah.

BIBLE PROMISE: 'God is our refuge and strength, an ever present help in trouble' (Psalm 46:1).

44 King Belshazzar of Babylon did a terrible thing. When the Babylonians captured Daniel and his friends, they also took back the gold and silver temple plates and goblets from Jerusalem and Belshazzar used them at a party where all sorts of things went on. God was not pleased!

The Lord wrote a message to Belshazzar on the wall where the party was being held and when Daniel translated it, it was not good news. King Belshazzar died that very night. (Daniel 5)

BIBLE PROMISE: Jesus said, 'All that the Father gives me will come to me, and whoever comes to me I will never drive away' (John 6:37).

45

Jesus told a story about two brothers. One stayed at home to work for his father, the other took his share of the family money and wasted every penny of it before returning home to ask his father to forgive him. The father was so delighted that he threw a welcome home party – but his older son was not amused! He stomped off in a temper.

Jesus told that story to show how welcome sinners are when they come to God asking for his forgiveness – but there's another lesson in there too! (Luke 15:11-32)

BIBLE PROMISE: The LORD says, 'So do not fear, for I am with you; do not be dismayed, for I am your God. I will strengthen you and help you; I will uphold you with my righteous right hand' (Isaiah 41:10).

46

Do you like picnics? A large crowd followed Jesus for several days to hear what he had to say. They were all outside in the open air. Jesus fed more than 5,000 people all from a few rolls and some little fish.

Why did he do that? The Bible tells us the answer. Jesus said, 'I have compassion for these people; they have already been with me three days and have nothing to eat. I do not want to send them away hungry, or they may collapse on the way.' (Matthew 14:13-21) Jesus knows all our needs because he made us.

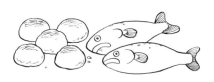

● ●

BIBLE PROMISE: God says, 'I will send down showers in season; there will be showers of blessing' (Ezekiel 34:26).

47 On the night before he died, Jesus and his friends met to celebrate the Passover. When the meal was finished the Lord gave his friends bread and wine as symbols (pictures) of his body and blood.

The bread was a picture of his body which was to be broken on the cross. The wine was a picture of his blood that was to be shed on the cross. Jesus then told his followers to remember him by sharing bread and wine in that way.

Christians still do that. They call it Communion or the Lord's Supper. (Matthew 26:17-29)

• •

BIBLE PROMISE: 'Delight yourself in the LORD and he will give you the desires of your heart' (Psalm 37:4).

48 After Jesus rose from the dead, he appeared early one morning to his friends who were out fishing in their boat. They had caught nothing all night. The Lord called to them, telling them where the fish were. Then the men caught so many that their nets nearly broke. But when they reached the shore, dragging their full nets behind them, the disciples discovered that Jesus already had fish cooking on a fire on the shore.

What a wonderful barbecue they must have had with the risen Lord! (John 21:1-14)

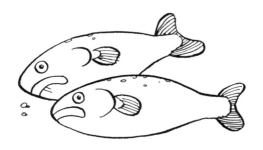

BIBLE PROMISE: 'Cast your cares on the Lᴏʀᴅ and he will sustain you; he will never let the righteous fall' (Psalm 55:22).

'Though your sins
are like scarlet,
they shall be
white as snow.'
(Isaiah 1:18)

TREES AND FORESTS

49 Adam and Eve had everything they needed or could want in the wonderful Garden of Eden. There was just one thing God told them not to do. '... you must not eat from the tree of the knowledge of good and evil, for when you eat of it you will surely die.' (Genesis 2:16). And what did they do? First Eve, and then Adam, ate the fruit of the forbidden tree. That was the very first sin, and we are still paying the price for it. That tree was one very serious temptation, and our first parents allowed themselves to give in to the temptation.

BIBLE PROMISE: '... by one sacrifice he (Jesus) has made perfect for ever those who are being made holy' (Hebrews 10:14).

50 Nothing was the same again. Even the earth was cursed by God because of the sin Adam and Eve had committed.

They were shut out of the Garden of Eden, never to return to it again. They were banished in order to keep them away from the tree of life. (Genesis 3:24) Had they eaten from the tree of life they would have lived forever as sinners. By keeping them away from it God allowed them time to be sorry, to ask for his forgiveness, and to go to heaven when they died.

In heaven, where everyone trusts in the Lord Jesus Christ, the tree of life stands where everyone can see it, and it bears twelve crops of fruit, one for every month of the year. (Revelation 22:2)

· ·

CHLOE'S QUESTIONS: Who were the first to see Jesus after he rose from the dead?

BIBLE PROMISE: 'If we confess our sins, he is faithful and just and will forgive us our sins and purify us from all unrighteousness' (1 John 1:9).

51

Remember Abraham and his wife Sarah? They longed for a baby even though they were very old. One day three angelic visitors came to see Abraham. They promised Abraham that he would have a baby boy in a year's time. Sarah overheard and laughed.

Where does a tree fit into that story? Abraham left his three visitors resting in the shade of a tree while he arranged their meal. (Genesis 18:1-15) That was kind of him, for the Bible tells us that they came in the hottest part of the day.

BIBLE PROMISE: 'You will again have compassion on us; you will tread our sins underfoot and hurl all our iniquities into the depths of the sea' (Micah 7:19).

52 The Hebrew people had some things that were very precious to them. They were the stone tablets on which God had written the Ten Commandments, a rod that had belonged to Aaron, the first High Priest and a pot of precious manna, the supernatural food with which God fed his people in the wilderness.

A special chest was made of acacia wood to hold these treasures. But nobody could see the wood of the acacia tree after the chest was finished for the whole thing was covered with pure gold both inside and out! The chest was called the ark of the covenant or the ark of the Lord. (Exodus 37:1-2)

•••

CHLOE'S QUESTIONS: Name two trees from the Garden of Eden.

BIBLE PROMISE: '"Come now, let us reason together," says the LORD. "Though your sins are like scarlet, they shall be white as snow; though they are red as crimson, they shall be like wool"' (Isaiah 1:18).

53

Some trees are especially good for building, and one of these is the cedar. It is tall and provides long planks of wood.

One day, when David was in his palace made of cedar wood, he had a mind-blowing thought. Here he was in a lovely palace while the ark of the Lord was just in a tent. He decided there and then that a wonderful temple should be built for it.

God had another plan. Because David had been a man of war the Lord wanted David's son Solomon to build the temple instead. (2 Samuel 7:1-2)

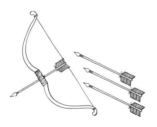

. . . .

BIBLE PROMISE: 'If the LORD delights in a man's way, he makes his steps firm; though he stumble, he will not fall, for the LORD upholds him with his hand' (Psalm 37:23-24).

54 Do you feel disappointed and resentful if there is something you really want to do and the pleasure goes to someone else? King David didn't. He immediately started gathering together materials for his son Solomon to use when he built the temple. That must have involved cutting down hundreds of trees, some of them olive trees to make the carved cherubim for the inner sanctuary and pine trees for the ornamental doors. (1 Kings 6:23 and 34)

· ·

BIBLE PROMISE: Jesus said, 'I am the light of the world. Whoever follows me will never walk in darkness, but will have the light of life' (John 8:12).

5 5 When Solomon started gathering wood to build the temple trees were felled in huge numbers. He sent for cedar logs from the King of Tyre and for algum (possibly juniper) logs too. He wanted so much wood that he promised to pay the woodmen who cut the timber 20,000 cors of wheat, 20,000 cors of barley, 20,000 baths of wine and 20,000 baths of olive oil! (A cor was about 220 litres. A bath was about 22 litres.)

Imagine counting out 20,000 of anything! (2 Chronicles 2:3, 8, 10)

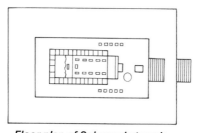

Floor plan of Solomon's temple

• •

BIBLE PROMISE: 'So we fix our eyes not on what is seen, but on what is unseen. For what is seen is temporary, but what is unseen is eternal' (2 Corinthians 4:18).

56

Sometimes King David was so filled with joy at the works of the Lord that he could do nothing but sing. In one of his psalms he even called on the trees of the forest to sing with joy before the Lord! (1 Chronicles 16:33)

There were sad times too. One of the psalms remembers when the Jews were in exile in Babylon. Their captors wanted them to sing the songs they had sung in Jerusalem. But what did they do? They hung up their harps on the branches of the nearby poplar trees because their hearts were so sad they didn't feel like singing at all. (Psalm 137:1-4)

● ●

BIBLE PROMISE: 'Blessed is he who has regard for the weak; the Lord delivers him in times of trouble' (Psalm 41:1).

57 Queen Esther was a brave young woman who saved the Jews from disaster by being a good queen to King Xerxes. An enemy of the Jews named Haman plotted to have Esther's Uncle Mordecai hanged. He even had a tree felled and gallows built for the job. Haman hated the Jews that much. But, thanks to Esther's courage, the king found out about it and the evil man was hung on his own gallows. (Esther 7:10)

Mordecai should have been shown respect. He had actually saved the king's life. To whom should we show respect? Sometimes old people are treated as though they are useless and don't really matter any more. That's not how God thinks. Many elderly Christians live such godly lives that people see the reflection of Jesus in them. (Psalm 92:12-15)

• •

BIBLE PROMISE: The LORD says, '… I will forgive their wickedness and will remember their sins no more' (Jeremiah 31:34).

5 8 Trees played a part in the life of Jesus, from his birth right through to his death. When he was born he was laid in a little wooden manger, made to hold cattle feed. When he died, he was crucified on a wooden cross, the saddest use to which God's creation was ever put. (Luke 2:16 and Acts 5:30)

Jesus knew more about wood than most boys because he was brought up by carpenter Joseph. (Matthew 13:55) No doubt Jesus played with left-over bits of wood as he watched his father working and later he became a carpenter himself.

● ●

CHLOE'S QUESTIONS: What was the name of the special box that the Hebrew people kept in the temple?

BIBLE PROMISE: '"You my sheep, the sheep of my pasture, are people, and I am your God," declares the Sovereign LORD' (Ezekiel 34:31).

59

Once, a blind man was brought to Jesus for healing. Jesus made clay, put it on the man's eyes, and asked if he could see anything. The man looked around but things seemed blurred to him. In fact, he said that people looked like trees walking! Once again Jesus touched his eyes and then the man could see clearly.

What's fascinating about that? It's the only miracle in the Bible that was done in two stages and we don't know why. (Mark 8:22-26)

• •

ABBI'S INFO: Here is a very strange Bible story. In order to be king, Abimelech had all but one of his brothers murdered. His one remaining brother gathered the people together and told them a story about trees discussing who should be most important. The story showed what a terrible man Abimelech was and what an awful king he would be. (Judges 9:1-25)

BIBLE PROMISE: 'Though I walk in the midst of trouble, you preserve my life; you stretch out your hand against the anger of my foes, with your right hand you save me' (Psalm 138:7).

73

6 0 Jesus told a story about good trees bearing good fruit and bad trees bearing bad fruit. The people must have smiled when he said that you couldn't pick figs from thorn bushes or grapes from briars. Of course you can't!

The meaning of Jesus' story is that our actions show the state of our hearts. (Luke 6:43-45)

• •

ABBI'S INFO: Adam and Eve were shut out of the Garden to keep them away from the tree of life. But in heaven, where everyone trusts in Christ, the tree of life stands where everyone can see it. (Revelation 22:2)

BIBLE PROMISE: 'No harm befalls the righteous, but the wicked have their fill of trouble' (Proverbs 12:21).

61

Children like climbing trees and looking down on people, but adults don't often do that.

Once, when Jesus was going through Jericho a man called Zacchaeus, who was not very tall, climbed up into a tree in order to see Jesus. He was not a popular man because he collected taxes for the Roman government. However, Jesus looked up and saw him and then invited himself in to Zacchaeus' home and heart. (Luke 19:1-10)

• •

BIBLE PROMISE: Jesus said, '... when you give to the needy, do not let your left hand know what your right hand is doing, so that your giving may be in secret. Then your Father, who sees what is done in secret, will reward you' (Matthew 6:3-4).

6 2 Jesus once said that he was like a tree, a vine tree. Not only that, he said that those who believe in him are like the branches! Only when branches are joined to the tree can they grow and flourish, and only when we are united to the Lord Jesus Christ will we grow and be fruitful believers. (John 15:1-8)

. . . .

BIBLE PROMISE: '"As for me, this is my covenant with them," says the LORD. "My Spirit who is on you, and my words that I have put in your mouth will not depart from your mouth, or from the mouths of your children, or from the mouths of their descendants from this time on and for ever," says the LORD' (Isaiah 59:21).

6 3 Just days before his death the Lord Jesus went up to Jerusalem, knowing full well what was about to happen. As he neared the city riding on a donkey, a crowd gathered and they cut branches off palm trees to spread on the road before him. They even threw their cloaks on the road for the Lord to ride over.

The people knew he was the special son of David that God had promised. That's why they cried, 'Hosanna!' to him. (Matthew 21:9)

• •

ABBI'S INFO: This incident in the life of Jesus was prophesied hundreds of years before in the Old Testament. Read Zechariah 9:9.

BIBLE PROMISE: 'For I will forgive their wickedness, and will remember their sins no more' (Hebrews 8:12).

64 The night before the Lord's death he went to the Mount of Olives to pray. It was in the shelter of these olive trees that he poured out all his sadness to his heavenly Father.

Jesus was a real man, and he didn't want to die on the cross. But because he knew that his death would mean that people like you and me could be saved and go to heaven, he prayed to his father, '... not my will, but yours be done.' (Luke 22:42)

• •

CHLOE'S QUESTIONS: How is Jesus like a tree and his followers like fruit?

BIBLE PROMISE: 'But with you there is forgiveness; therefore you are feared' (Psalm 130:4).

'The LORD your God is with you, he is mighty to save.'
(Zephaniah 3:17)

FASCINATING FAMILIES

65 Bible families are just like families today, with all their fun and arguments, love and hate, and disappointment. One family was special, the very first family of all.

After God made the first man and woman, he blessed them and told them to be fruitful and increase in number. Imagine Adam and Eve's delight, surprise and excitement when their first baby was born, the first baby ever.

Tragically, their son would also be the first ever murderer, for he murdered his very own brother. (Genesis 1:28, 4:8)

• •

CHLOE'S QUESTIONS: Can you think of a time when Jesus describes himself as something you eat?

BIBLE PROMISE: Paul said, 'Here is a trustworthy saying that deserves full acceptance: Christ Jesus came into the world to save sinners – of whom I am the worst' (1 Timothy 1:15).

66 Abraham and Sarah waited a very, very long time before God gave them a baby. It's not surprising that when their son Isaac grew up his father wanted to find a good wife for him. He wanted the very best for his son.

Parents want the best for their children because they love them, and the very best that any parent can pray for is that their sons and daughters will trust in the Lord Jesus as their Saviour. (Genesis 24:1-4)

BIBLE PROMISE: 'God called you to this (to be saved) through our gospel, that you might share in the glory of our Lord Jesus Christ (2 Thessalonians 2:14).

6 7 Although Isaac and Rebekah loved each other, they were not very wise. They had twin boys called Jacob and Esau and they were unwise enough to have favourites. Esau was Jacob's favourite son and Jacob was Rebekah's favourite son. Of course, the boys didn't get on, and after a major battle over Jacob cheating his brother, he had to run away for his life.

Favouritism is really, really stupid and always causes problems! (Genesis 25:28)

BIBLE PROMISE: Jesus said, 'Blessed are those who are persecuted because of righteousness, for theirs is the kingdom of heaven' (Matthew 5:10).

68

Jacob grew up and fell in love. But, having been a cheat himself, he was outdone in cheating by his father-in-law who married him off to the wrong daughter! She was called Leah. Eventually Jacob also married her sister, Rachel, whom he loved.

Jacob had twelve sons, the first ten with Leah and the last two with Rachel. And guess what ... he had a favourite, Joseph, Rachel's first son. You would have thought that Jacob would have learned his lesson! (Genesis 37:3)

BIBLE PROMISE: 'The LORD your God is with you, he is mighty to save. He will take great delight in you, he will quiet you with his love, he will rejoice over you with singing' (Zephaniah 3:17).

69

Generations in a family often repeat the same mistakes. Jacob had to run away to prevent Esau killing him and in the next generation Jacob's ten oldest sons sold Joseph instead of killing him. What a family! (Genesis 37:12-36)

Although it often happens, generations in a family need not repeat the same mistakes. With God's help bad patterns can be broken. Although Joseph was his father's favourite there is no mention of him having a favourite between his two sons. (Genesis 48:8-21)

● ●

ZAC'S CHALLENGE: Jacob had several wives, twelve sons and one daughter. Look up Genesis 35 and draw a family tree for Jacob with his parents, grandparents, his wives and children.

BIBLE PROMISE: 'For the LORD will not reject his people; he will never forsake his inheritance' (Psalm 94:14).

70

Moses' parents loved their little son too much to obey evil Pharaoh's law and drown him in the River Nile. And they loved and trusted their daughter so much that they gave her the job of looking after her baby brother tucked up in his basket among the reeds. (Exodus 2:1-10)

That's what families should be about – loving and trusting and caring for each other.

. . . .

BIBLE PROMISE: 'Jesus Christ is the same yesterday and today and forever' (Hebrews 13:8).

7 1 Moses and Aaron were brothers. They were good at different things, as all brothers are. When God told Moses that he was to go to evil Pharaoh and tell him to set the Hebrew people free from their slavery, Moses immediately said that he couldn't do it, that he didn't have the gift of speaking. God allowed Moses to take his brother with him and for them to do the Lord's work together. (Exodus 6:28–7:2)

Here we see two brothers getting on well and working together. It can be done!

●●●●●●●●●●●●●●●●●●●●●●●●●●●●●●●●●

CHLOE'S QUESTIONS: Who was Rebekah's favourite son and who was Isaac's favourite?

BIBLE PROMISE: God says, 'My grace is sufficient for you, for my power is made perfect in weakness' (2 Corinthians 12:9).

72

Did you know that two of the Ten Commandments are about families? The fifth Commandment says, 'Honour your father and your mother, so that you may live long in the land the Lord your God is giving you.' And by honouring our parents we honour the Lord our God who told us to do so. (Exodus 20:12)

The Seventh Commandment is also about families. 'You shall not commit adultery.' A married man should only have eyes for his wife, and a married woman should only have eyes for her husband. God gave them to each other until they are parted by death. If the Seventh Commandment were kept there would be many fewer broken hearts in our world today. (Exodus 20:14)

BIBLE PROMISE: Jesus said, 'For where two or three come together in my name, there am I with them' (Matthew 18:20).

73

Do your parents ever speak to you about the Lord? If they do, they are doing just exactly what God told them to do.

This is what the Bible says. 'Love the Lord your God with all your heart and with all your soul and with all your strength. These commandments that I give you today are to be upon your hearts. Impress them on your children. Talk about them when you sit at home and when you walk along the road, when you lie down and when you get up.' (Deuteronomy 6:5-7)

• •

BIBLE PROMISE: God says, 'Now if you obey me fully and keep my covenant, then out of all nations you will be my treasured possession' (Exodus 19:5).

7 4 As you grow older and more independent, you may think that your parents should not 'interfere' in your life. That's what Samson must have thought, when his father and mother objected to him marrying someone who didn't believe in God. (Judges 14:1-3)

Was Samson right to do what he did? You'll be able to work out the answer from 2 Corinthians 6:14-16, but you'll need to think about it.

• •
BIBLE PROMISE: Paul says, 'Whatever you have learned or received or heard from me, or seen in me – put into practice. And the God of peace will be with you' (Philippians 4:9).

75

One of the shortest books in the Bible is Ruth, and it is a love story. Naomi's husband and two sons died, leaving her with two daughters-in-law, neither of whom had children. What a sad little trio of women. One went back to her parents, but the other – that was Ruth – admired and loved her mother-in-law so much that she promised always to stay with her. She did.

Later Ruth married again and had a son. That was all part of God's great plan and her son was a great, great, many times great grandfather of the Lord Jesus Christ! (The Book of Ruth is found between Judges and 1 Samuel.)

• •

BIBLE PROMISE: Jesus said, 'If you obey my commands, you will remain in my love, just as I have obeyed my Father's commands and remain in his love' (John 15:10).

76 In Old Testament times men often had many wives. Elkanah had two wives. One had children and the other, Hannah, had not. Over time she became quite desperate to have a child and her husband's other wife was just horrid to her. (1 Samuel 1:6)

Do you ever tease someone who doesn't have all that you have? God doesn't like that.

ABBI'S INFO: In the Bible, God gives rules to parents and children. Children are told to obey their parents in the Lord and fathers are told not to exasperate their children. (Ephesians 6:1, 4)

BIBLE PROMISE: 'The way of the LORD is a refuge for the righteous, but it is the ruin of those who do evil' (Proverbs 10:29).

77

One day Hannah was praying so hard for a baby that the temple priest thought she was drunk! God knew she was praying and heard and answered her prayer by giving her a little baby boy. His name was Samuel. Hannah was not a possessive mother. When Samuel was old enough, she took him to the temple where he was trained to serve the Lord God. (1 Samuel 1:27-28)

Sometimes parents try to hang on to their children, even trying to stop them from answering God's call to be missionaries. If you are a Christian, and your parents are not, try to be gentle with them and pray that they will come to faith in Jesus.

• •

BIBLE PROMISE: '"Because he loves me," says the LORD, "I will rescue him; I will protect him, for he acknowledges my name. He will call upon me, and I will answer him; I will be with him in trouble, I will deliver him and honour him."' (Psalm 91:14-15).

78

The prophet Samuel was sent by God to a man named Jesse because the Lord was calling one of Jesse's sons to be the next king of Israel. Samuel looked at every son in the family, from the oldest one down. And they were an impressive set of men, strong, handsome and brave. But God had chosen the youngest son to be king. (1 Samuel 16:7)

God looks on the heart and not on the outward appearance.

BIBLE PROMISE: Jesus said, 'If you remain in me and my words remain in you, ask whatever you wish, and it will be given you' (John 15:7).

79 King David was a great king, and a great man of God. But he was not perfect. In fact, he did a terrible thing that destroyed a whole family. He fell in love with a woman who was already married and then arranged for her husband to be killed in battle so that he could marry her. What a despicable thing to do! (2 Samuel 11)

Amazingly, God forgave David and was still able to use him. And he is able to forgive us, whatever we have done, and to use us in the work of his kingdom. Wonderful!

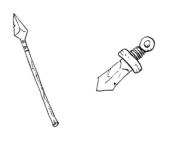

● ●

BIBLE PROMISE: 'As a mother comforts her child, so will I comfort you' (Isaiah 66:13).

80 One of David's sons, Absalom, gave his father a really bad time. He was as awful to him as King Saul had been. Despite that, when news reached David of Absalom's death, the king was so brokenhearted that he said he wished he'd died himself instead of his sinful son. Parents sometimes put up with a lot, but good parents never stop loving their children (2 Samuel 18:33).

Do your parents ever give you advice? I'm sure they do! When the time was coming for David to die, he gave his son Solomon some advice. 'Be strong, show yourself a man, and observe what the Lord your God requires; Walk in his ways, and keep his decrees and commands.' That was the best fatherly advice of all. (1 Kings 2:2-3)

• •
BIBLE PROMISE: 'If you return to the Almighty, you will be restored' (Job 22:23).

81

Jesus was part of an ordinary human family. Some people believe that he was an only child, but that's not what the Bible says. Those who knew him said, 'Isn't this the carpenter's son? Isn't his mother's name Mary, and aren't his brothers James, Joseph, Simon and Judas? Aren't all his sisters with us?'

Jesus knows all about family life from the inside, and he understands the joys and sorrows, the stresses and strains. (Matthew 13:55-56)

• •

BIBLE PROMISE: 'Set your minds on things above, not on earthly things. For you died, and your life is now hidden with Christ in God. When Christ, who is your life, appears, then you also will appear with him in glory' (Colossians 3:2-4).

8 2 Do you sometimes feel that your family doesn't understand you at all? Jesus knows exactly how you feel. There was even a terrible time in his life when his brothers thought he was out of his mind.

But Jesus said a wonderful thing about family. 'Whoever does God's will is my brother and sister and mother.' Following the Lord Jesus is really and truly to be part of his family. (Mark 3:35) And the reason that is true is that God adopts those who are given the gift of faith in Jesus. '… to those who believed in his name, he gave the right to become children of God.'

Think about it. Every single Christian is an adopted child of God! That's why they can call him their heavenly Father. How amazing is that? (John 1:12)

● ●

BIBLE PROMISE: 'Serve him with wholehearted devotion and with a willing mind, for the LORD searches every heart and understands every desire and every thought. If you seek him, he will be found by you; but if you forsake him, he will reject you forever' (1 Chronicles 28:9).

83

The Christian family is a real family, so much so that, if someone helps lead another person to faith in Jesus, he is sometimes known as his father or mother in the faith. So Paul, when he wrote to Timothy, was able to call him his true son in the faith because he had helped to lead Timothy to Jesus. (1 Timothy 1:2)

• •

BIBLE PROMISE: 'The righteous lead blameless lives; blessed are their children after them' (Proverbs 20:7).

BiBLE BUiLDiNGS

84

There are some really impressive building projects in the Bible. Here we have one that was God's idea and the next fact is about another one that was thought up by some very foolish men.

When Noah was told by God to build an ark, he had no idea what a building project it would be. The ark needed to be massive because it was to be used to save eight members of Noah's family and two or more of each of all the animals and birds. (Genesis 6:15)

• •

ABBI'S INFO: How big was the ark? Noah was told to build it 450 feet long, 75 feet wide and 45 feet high – that's the height of seven tall men standing on top of each other! That's big.

BIBLE PROMISE: 'No one will be able to stand against you all the days of your life. As I was with Moses, so I will be with you; I will never leave you nor forsake you' (Joshua 1:5).

85 In the beginning only one language was spoken and everyone understood it. Some men decided to build a huge tower called Babel, a tower as high as the clouds. Because the people all spoke the same language they were able to plan the project.

When God saw that people were beginning to think they could do anything they liked, he made them speak different languages. Of course, they couldn't understand one another! When that happened the builders couldn't work together and the project was abandoned. From Babel the different language groups spread over the world and became different nations. (Genesis 11:1-9)

● ●

ZAC'S CHALLENGE: What parts of your body are used in communication? Look up these verses: Ephesians 4:29; Matthew 11:15; 1 Corinthians 2:9; Psalm 66:6. What body parts are mentioned?

BIBLE PROMISE: 'When the LORD takes pleasure in anyone's way, he causes their enemies to make peace with them' (Proverbs 16:7).

86

Moses was told by God to make a tent (called the tabernacle) which was to go everywhere with the children of Israel as they travelled. It was to house the ark of the Lord, and was to be pitched wherever they camped. Read Exodus 36:8-38 to discover how intricate it was.

God gave the exact measurements for every part, even telling Moses what woods and metals to use. Much of the woodwork was overlaid with gold. Nothing is too good for God.

• •

BIBLE PROMISE: 'The Lord knows how to rescue the godly from trials and to hold the unrighteous for punishment on the day of judgment' (2 Peter 2:9).

87

When God's people reached the Promised Land after their forty years in the wilderness, Joshua sent two men to spy out the city of Jericho.

A woman named Rahab had lived a bad life, but she changed and helped the spies. The King of Jericho sent out search parties. Rahab's house, which had a flat roof, was built into the city wall. She hid the spies on her roof underneath piles of flax stalks that were laid out to dry. When the King's men had gone, she let the spies down by a rope through her window on the outside of the city wall and they escaped. (Joshua 2)

• •

ABBI'S INFO: Rahab was not a Hebrew, but she joined the Hebrew people and became one of them through marriage. She features in the family tree of King David and through that the family tree of Jesus too!

BIBLE PROMISE: 'Great peace have those who love your law, and nothing can make them stumble' (Psalm 119:165).

88 The city of Jericho had been strongly built and was not easily invaded. But God gave it to his people without so much as them firing an arrow!

He told Joshua and his armed men to march round the city once a day for six days. Seven priests were to accompany them carrying rams' horn trumpets as they walked in front of the ark of the Lord. On the seventh day, they had to march around Jericho seven times with the priests blowing their trumpets.

The people inside Jericho must have wondered what was going on. They were about to find out! After their seventh walk right round Jericho the people gave a loud shout and the city walls collapsed. The Hebrew people charged in and took the city. Jericho was burned down but Rahab and her family were saved. (Joshua 6)

• •

BIBLE PROMISE: 'The LORD has heard my cry for mercy; the LORD accepts my prayer' (Psalm 6:9).

89

Elisha was one of God's prophets and he travelled all over the country telling the people what the Lord wanted them to know. Of course, he got to know people on his travels.

One such couple lived in Shumen and Elisha had a meal with them each time he went there. The wife, who knew he was a man of God, suggested that they build a little room on the flat roof of their house and furnish it with a bed, a table, a chair and a lamp for Elisha to use each time he was passing. (2 Kings 4:8-10)

•••••••••••••••••••••••••••••••••••••••

BIBLE PROMISE: 'The LORD will be king over the whole earth. On that day there will be one LORD, and his name the only name' (Zechariah 14:9)

90

A very amazing thing happened in that little room some time later.

The couple had a son who suddenly took ill and died. His mother put the dead child up in the prophet's room and rushed off to find Elisha. When he heard what had happened, Elisha went as quickly as he could to her home and climbed the stairs up to his room.

Closing the door behind him, the prophet prayed for the boy. Then he did a strange thing. He lay on top of the child, warming the dead body with the heat of his own body. After he did that for a second time, the boy sneezed and opened his eyes.

God answered Elisha's prayer and gave the child his life back again. (2 Kings 4:18-36)

• •

BIBLE PROMISE: 'Have no fear of sudden disaster or of the ruin that overtakes the wicked, for the LORD will be at your side and will keep your foot from being snared' (Proverbs 3:25-26).

91 God gave King Solomon the job of building the temple in Jerusalem, and what a temple it was! It took seven years to complete the three storey high building.

Among the workforce who brought materials from different countries as well as working on the building itself were 30,000 men who went in shifts to Lebanon, 70,000 carriers, 80,000 stone cutters as well as 33,000 foremen who supervised the project and told the workmen what to do. The finished temple must have been absolutely magnificent. (2 Chronicles chapters 3 to 5)

Having completed the temple, you would have thought that Solomon would have had enough of building to last his whole life. Not at all. The next thirteen years were spent erecting a royal palace. (2 Chronicles 7:11)

• •

BIBLE PROMISE: 'The Sovereign LORD is my strength; he makes my feet like the feet of a deer, he enables me to tread on the heights' (Habakkuk 3:19).

92 God's chosen people were often disobedient and sometimes he had to punish them to help them see sense. Once, they were punished by being overrun by the Babylonians who took most of the people back home with them, leaving Jerusalem to fall into ruins.

Some years later Nehemiah, who worked for the King of Babylon, was brokenhearted when he heard the state of Jerusalem and he obtained permission from the king to go back there and organise the rebuilding of its walls. It was a huge job – but it was completed in just fifty-two days because everyone worked so hard. (Nehemiah 6:15) The Book of Nehemiah is an exciting read.

• •

ABBI'S INFO: When you have a problem, there are two things you can do. Pray to God and do your best. (Nehemiah 4:9)

BIBLE PROMISE: 'Jesus replied, "But I say to all of you: From now on you will see the Son of Man sitting at the right hand of the Mighty One and coming on the clouds of heaven"' (Matthew 26:64).

93

Daniel was a captive in Babylon, one of a group of specially gifted Hebrew young people whom the Babylonians wanted to train up to work for them. The king tried to make them more Babylonian than the Babylonians. His project was a complete failure with Daniel and his friends.

Years later, King Nebuchadnezzar built a huge image of gold which he insisted that everyone should worship. Daniel's friends would have none of it; they only worshipped the one true God. Because of that Daniel's friends were put inside a special Babylonian building – a burning fiery furnace! God was with them and kept them safe in the flames. (Daniel 3)

• •

ABBI'S INFO: When Daniel's friends were brought out of the fiery furnace, they didn't even smell of smoke!

BIBLE PROMISE: 'Come near to God and he will come near to you' (James 4:8).

94

Another king came to the Babylonian throne and he too wanted to be God. He passed a law that all prayers had to be said to him. Daniel refused to do that! Instead, he went into his house to the upstairs room in which he usually prayed. The windows faced Jerusalem, which must have felt very far away to Daniel, and he knelt and prayed to the Lord.

Spies reported back to the king and Daniel was put into a den of hungry lions. God closed the lions' mouths and Daniel was totally unharmed. (Daniel 6:1-23)

• •

BIBLE PROMISE: 'When you lie down, you will not be afraid; when you lie down, your sleep will be sweet' (Proverbs 3:24)

95

We go to another upper room now, where something quite different was happening.

It was the night before Jesus died on the cross and he and his friends met in an upstairs room in a house in Jerusalem. After celebrating the Passover meal together, Jesus gave his friends bread and wine. That was the very first Communion service. From there Jesus went to Gethsemane to pray. While he was in the garden he was captured and then taken to be tried and sentenced to death. (Luke 22)

ABBI'S INFO: Closed doors are no barrier to the Lord, and neither are closed hearts. If someone you love seems to have a closed heart and mind towards Christian things, keep praying for God is still able to save. (Mark 14:13-26)

BIBLE PROMISE: 'Worship the Lord your God, and his blessing will be on your food and water' (Exodus 23:25).

96

After he rose from the dead, Jesus appeared to his friends on several occasions. Once they were in a locked room in a house because Jesus' followers were so scared. Even though the door was locked Jesus entered the room and comforted his friends. (Luke 24:36)

Not long afterwards the friends of Jesus were very different. Instead of being filled with fear they were filled with God's Holy Spirit, and all because of what happened on the Day of Pentecost.

They were gathered together, scared as usual, when the Holy Spirit was sent from heaven like a violent wind and the very house shook. What looked like tongues of fire rested on their heads and they were able to speak in different languages! Jesus' friends were no longer scared. They went outside to tell what had happened and people were able to understand them wherever they came from! (Acts 2:1-13)

• •

BIBLE PROMISE: 'And everyone who calls on the name of the Lord will be saved' (Joel 2:32).

97

Paul, who became a Christian after the death and resurrection of the Lord Jesus, was one of the church's early missionaries. He and Silas took the good news of Jesus to the city of Philippi and were locked up in the town's prison for doing so! Not only that, but their feet were fastened in the stocks.

At midnight, while the two Christians were praying and singing hymns, God sent such a severe earthquake that all the prisoners' chains fell loose and the prison doors swung open! The jailor thought that his prisoners had escaped and was about to kill himself when Paul stopped him.

By the end of that exciting night the jailor and all his family had become Christians! (Acts 16:16-40)

• •

CHLOE'S QUESTIONS: Who built the temple in Jerusalem and who wanted to build it?

BIBLE PROMISE: 'A generous person will prosper; whoever refreshes others will be refreshed' (Proverbs 11:25).

114

98

We next find the missionaries in Troas on the third storey of a building where Paul was preaching. The room was warmed by lamps and human bodies.

A young man, called Eutychus, sat on the windowsill to listen. Around midnight Eutychus dozed off and fell out of the window to his death. When Paul went down to him God gave the young man back his life. What did Paul do then? He went back upstairs and continued speaking! (Acts 20:7-12)

· ·

ABBI'S INFO: Paul wrote most of the letters (epistles) in the New Testament. Some were written from prisons. His prison life was part of his mission as some of those who worked for Caesar were converted! (Philippians 4:22)

BIBLE PROMISE: 'In that day I will make a covenant for them with the beasts of the field, the birds in the sky and the creatures that move along the ground. Bow and sword and battle I will abolish from the land, so that all may lie down in safety' (Hosea 2:18).

99

The last place mentioned in the Bible is even more wonderful than Solomon's temple could ever have been. It is the Holy City, the New Jerusalem, a picture of which was given by God as a vision to John.

It is too glorious even to begin to describe, but all those who trust in the Lord Jesus will one day have their eternal home there, and all God's people will be with him. (Revelation 21:3)

ZAC'S CHALLENGE: Read Revelation 21 and draw a picture of every kind of precious stone mentioned in the chapter. You might have to do some research to find out what colours these are!

BIBLE PROMISE: '... the Lord's unfailing love surrounds the one who trusts in him' (Psalm 32:10).

'The LORD will guide you always.'
(Isaiah 58:11)

HEAVEN - WHAT ABOUT iT?

100 God the Father is in heaven. We know that because the Lord Jesus taught us to pray, 'Our Father in heaven, hallowed be your name ...' (Matthew 6:9).

The Lord Jesus Christ, who is the Lamb of God, reigns in heaven from his kingly throne. 'To him who sits on the throne and to the Lamb be praise and honour and glory and power, for ever and ever' (Revelation 5:13).

Thousands upon thousands of angels sing praises to the Lord Jesus in heaven. John, who was given a vision of heaven, saw them circling Christ's throne. He even heard the words of the song they were singing. 'Worthy is the Lamb, who was slain, to receive power and wealth and wisdom and strength and honour and glory and praise!' (Revelation 5:11-12)

● ●

BIBLE PROMISE: 'All these blessings will come upon you and accompany you if you obey the LORD your God: You will be blessed in the city and blessed in the country' (Deuteronomy 28:2-3).

101

John also saw people in heaven, so many that no-one could count them. They were from every nation, tribe, people and language. In his vision they were all standing in front of the Lamb on the throne. (Revelation 7:9)

Now, there is something very special about this crowd. John's vision was of how heaven will be at the end of time, so he caught a glimpse of all who will be there for eternity. That means, if you trust in the Lord Jesus Christ, you were in the crowd that John saw in his vision! Wow!

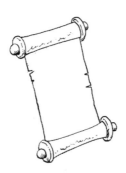

• •

BIBLE PROMISE: 'But as for me, I watch in hope for the LORD, I wait for God my Saviour; my God will hear me' (Micah 7:7).

102 The glory of the Lord Jesus is more than enough to light the whole of heaven. (Revelation 22:5) Our souls and bodies will be united forever when the Lord Jesus comes back in glory, and our heavenly bodies will be absolutely perfect and totally unable to be poorly or to feel pain. Of course, because all God's people are given the gift of eternal life, their heavenly bodies will never die. (John 3:16 and Revelation 21:4).

Because there is no death in heaven there will be no mourning and no tears. Imagine a place where no tears will ever be shed – that's heaven! (Revelation 21:4)

• •

BIBLE PROMISE: 'Do not be afraid of them, for I am with you and will rescue you," declares the LORD' (Jeremiah 1:8).

103

All God's people will be in heaven with him. None will be left behind and none will be missed out. Everyone for whom Christ died will spend eternity with him. Because God is all-powerful, his will IS done. Every single one of his people will be in heaven in that great day that will go on for ever and ever and ... ever! (Romans 8:29-30)

No matter how hard we try, as long as we remain on earth we will commit sin. Amazingly, when we go to heaven we will be made perfect. In fact, the Bible tells us that we will be like Jesus! (1 John 3:2)

And the best thing of all about heaven is that there we will see Jesus face to face and we will spend forever in his glorious company. How wonderful that will be! (1 John 3:2)

BIBLE PROMISE: 'The LORD will guide you always' (Isaiah 58:11.)

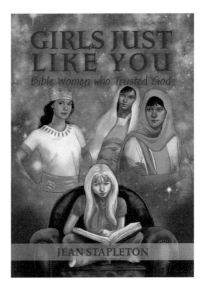

Girls just like you
by Jean Stapleton

We might think that people in Bible times were different from us (much braver and better than we are), but that isn't true. They were just like us – just like you, in fact! There are fifty different stories in this book, with Bible verses to read that will teach you about the girls and women in the Bible who trusted God. Find out about them and about yourself by discovering God's Word that He has written for you!

ISBN: 978-1-78191-997-2

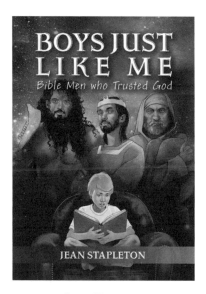

Boys just like me
by Jean Stapleton

We might think that people in Bible times were different from us (much braver and better than we are), but that isn't true. They were just like us – just like you, in fact! There are fifty different stories in this book, with Bible verses to read that will teach you about the boys and men in the Bible who trusted God. Find out about them and about yourself by discovering God's Word that He has written for you!

ISBN: 978-1-78191-998-9

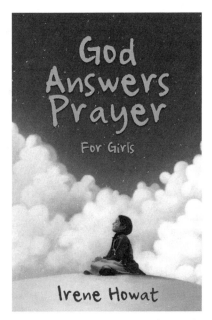

God Answers Prayer for Girls
by Irene Howat

Sisters and friends, mothers and daughters – they're all in this book and they all have one thing in common – they've prayed to the one true God – the God who always answers.

ISBN: 978-1-78191-151-8

God Answers Prayer for Boys
by Irene Howat

Brothers and friends, fathers and sons – they're all in this book and they all have one thing in common – they've prayed to the one true God – the God who always answers.

ISBN: 978-1-78191-152-5

CHRISTIAN FOCUS PUBLICATIONS

Christian Focus · Christian Heritage · CF4K · Mentor

Christian Focus Publications publishes books for adults and children under its four main imprints: Christian Focus, CF4K, Mentor and Christian Heritage. Our books reflect our conviction that God's Word is reliable and Jesus is the way to know him, and live for ever with him.

Our children's publication list includes a Sunday School curriculum that covers pre-school to early teens, and puzzle and activity books. We also publish personal and family devotional titles, biographies and inspirational stories that children will love.

If you are looking for quality Bible teaching for children then we have an excellent range of Bible stories and age-specific theological books.

From pre-school board books to teenage apologetics, we have it covered!

**Find us at our web page:
www.christianfocus.com**

CF4·K
Because you're never
too young to know Jesus